on the
radar

police forensics

Adam Sutherland

Lerner Publications Company

Minneapolis

Lerner Publications Company
A division of Lerner Publishing Group, Inc.
241 First Avenue North
Minneapolis, MN U.S.A.

Website address: www.lernerbooks.com

Library of Congress Cataloging-in-Publication Data

Sutherland, Adam.
    Police forensics / by Adam Sutherland.
      p.   cm. — (On the radar: defend and
protect)
    Includes index.
    ISBN 978–0–7613–7774–0 (lib. bdg. : alk. paper)
    1. Forensic sciences—Juvenile literature.
2. Criminal investigation—Juvenile literature.
I. Title.
HV8073.8.S88 2012
363.25—dc23   2011031685

Manufactured in the United States of America
– CG – 12/31/11

Acknowledgments: Corbis: Ocean 4, Sean Justice 12tr;
Dreamstime: Andresr 2tl, 17tr, BlueVision 27, Photowitch
3tr; iStock: Brandom Alms 14-15, CandyBox Photography
2c, 18–19, EdStock 10–11, Giorgio Fochesato 10cl, Peter
Kim 6, 27l, Mikkel William Nielsen 24, Jonathan Parry 28bl,
David Waugh 26; Science Photolibrary: Tek Image 11tr,
Jim Varney 20–21; Shutterstock: Aquatic Creature 2–3,
28–29, Arindambanerjee 25, Kevin L Chesson 3br, 13bl,
22bl, Corepics cover, Edw 5l, Fotohunter 2tr, 30–31, Shawn
Hempel 13cl, Robert Kneschke 1, Leigh 22tr, Luxorphoto 2br,
9tr, Loren Rodgers 16–17, 28br, Stocksnapp 26r, Leah-Anne
Thompson 29br, Almog Ziv 22tl; Wikimedia: 8, 9bl, 9tl.

Main body text set in
Helvetica Neue LT Std 13/15.5.
Typeface provided by Adobe Systems.

cover stories

thepeople

theskills

thetalk

Creepy-crawly clues

Forensic entomology is the study of insects and the information they can provide about a crime. For example, the type of insects found on or in the body of a murder victim can tell an entomologist approximately when the victim died.

CRACKING THE CASE

Forensic science is the use of science to solve crimes. Forensic experts collect evidence linked to a crime. Then they examine it in a laboratory to provide information that helps the police to solve the crime. There are many areas of forensics.

DRUGS AND CRIME

Forensic toxicology is the study of drugs and their effects on the body. By examining a person's blood, urine, or hair, it is possible to identify drugs or other toxins that the person may have used or been given.

THE CRIMINAL MIND

Forensic psychology looks at how and why people commit crimes. This area also studies how stress or emotional problems can lead to a person committing a crime.

HOW PEOPLE DIE

Forensic pathology is used to find out how and why a person died. The body is thoroughly examined during an autopsy to try to establish the cause of death.

WRITTEN CLUES

Forensic graphology looks at handwriting and its relation to crime. A graphologist examines a person's writing to find out more about the person's character and possible behavior.

TALKING TEETH

Forensic dentistry examines teeth. The exams can be used to identify the victim of a crime or the identity of a criminal who might have been bitten by the victim.

CRIME LAB VOCAB

Crack the language of crime scene forensics with the On the Radar guide.

antigen
the molecules in the body that help the immune system fight disease or repair itself after injury

autopsy
the examination of a body to find out the cause of death

ballistics
the science behind firearms and how they are used in a crime

case files
a collection of information put together by the police and police forensic teams on every crime that is investigated

cleanroom suit
a disposable paper suit worn by crime scene investigators to prevent fibers from their own clothes contaminating a crime scene

contaminate
to bring an outside source, such as extra fingerprints or the fibers from a jacket, into a crime scene. If the outside source mixes with the real evidence, it will confuse results and make it harder to find the criminal.

crime scene
the place where a crime took place

evidence
any information that can lead to catching a criminal

exposing reagent
a chemical that can be added to a substance to make something visible that would normally be invisible

hair follicle
the part of the hair that grows under the skin

infrared light
a type of light that can detect heat sources, including skin cells

latent prints
fingerprints that are usually left by accident and may not be immediately visible to the naked human eye

luminol
a chemical that is used by forensic investigators to detect blood at crime scenes where no blood is visible to the naked eye

Print examiners check evidence both at the crime scene and within the forensic lab for signs of prints.

patent prints

fingerprints that are clear and obvious to the human eye

print examiner

a forensic expert who specializes in studying fingerprints

serologist

someone who specializes in collecting blood and bodily fluid as evidence

serology

the study of blood

shell casings

the outer bullet covering that is left behind when a bullet is fired

toxins

poisons that may be present in the body

trace evidence

the evidence that occurs when two objects touch each other. For example, when two people shake hands, they both collect very small traces of each other's DNA.

ultraviolet light

a light that is invisible to the human eye and that can cause certain substances, including blood, to become visible

GLOSSARY

database

a computerized list of information that can include people's names, addresses, blood groups, and past criminal history

death row

in a prison, the area where prisoners who are sentenced to death await execution

defense attorneys

lawyers who are acting on behalf of the suspect of a crime, rather than the victim of a crime

DNA

short for deoxyribonucleic acid. DNA is the hereditary material in humans and almost all other organisms.

exiled

forced to live away from his or her home country

fictional

not real; made up

fraud

pretending that something is real when it is not

hacking

unauthorized entry into a computer network or a website

Nobel Prize

a prize awarded to people for their outstanding contribution in their particular field of work. The prize was established by a famous Swedish scientist, Alfred Nobel.

re-create

to make something look like the original

scan

to look at something closely

secure

to close off, or not allow entry to, a specific area

THE STORY OF CRIME DETECTION

The first forensic scientist was a fictional detective named Sherlock Holmes. Created by Sir Arthur Conan Doyle, a Scottish doctor turned author, Holmes used the science of fingerprinting and blood analysis to solve crimes. In the first Sherlock Holmes novel, *A Study in Scarlet*, published in 1887, Holmes developed a chemical that could tell if a stain was blood or not.

Sherlock Holmes, the world-famous fictional forensic scientist, has appeared in novels, comics *(above)*, and many films.

REAL-LIFE FORENSICS

Austrian-born professor Hans Gross was the world's first real-life forensic scientist. In 1893 he published the first handbook of forensics. He applied science to crime detection and introduced new areas, such as crime scene photography. In 1901 the biologist Karl Landsteiner first discovered that human blood could be separated into groups. He created the blood-identification system that is still in use.

THE TRANSFER SYSTEM

In 1910 a French doctor named Edmond Locard realized that everyone constantly picks up and leaves behind traces of their environment—dust, hair, threads from clothes, paint, and mud. Locard's Exchange Principle is the reason why all crime scenes are secured as soon as possible.

U.S. CRIME LABS

The first U.S. forensic lab was set up in 1923 by August Vollmer, who worked for the Los Angeles Police Department. The first private forensic lab was created in Chicago, Illinois, in 1929 as a result of a fight between rival criminal gangs that killed seven men. Calvin Goddard, the forensic scientist in charge of the case, was able to link the killings to crime leader Al Capone's gang by identifying exactly which guns had been used. In 1932 Goddard helped the Federal Bureau of Investigation (FBI) set up a national forensic laboratory, which could investigate cases on behalf of every police force in the United States.

Francis Crick (top) and James Watson (bottom) were awarded a Nobel Prize in 1962 for their contribution to science.

Unique identities

In 1953 two scientists, Francis Crick and James Watson, discovered the structure of DNA (the inherited traits in humans). In 1985 researchers proved that, except for some identical twins, each person's DNA is unique. A process called DNA typing was developed to highlight the differences in each person's DNA. Forensic scientists are able to take DNA samples from subjects by rubbing a cotton swab on the inside of the person's cheek and storing the information on a worldwide database.

EXPERTS ON-SITE

When a crime has been committed, a forensic team is sent to the scene as soon as possible. Team members examine and collect evidence that could prove essential to catching the criminal. Success is all about teamwork. Lots of people are involved, all doing different jobs.

PROTECTING THE SCENE

The police secure the scene. That means not allowing anyone in or out, so that evidence is not damaged. They also record everything that happens at the scene.

IN CHARGE OF THE BODY

The forensic investigator is in charge of a crime scene when a body has been found—for example, in a murder case. He or she is also the person who examines the body at a hospital.

COLLECTING EVIDENCE

Crime scene investigators collect evidence and take it to the lab. They draw and photograph the crime scene and take measurements so they can re-create the scene back at the lab.

FINDING THE WEAPON

If a gun has been used, a firearms, or ballistics, expert will become involved. This specialist looks at any guns and bullet holes found and collects bullets and shell casings. The expert also searches for the tiny amounts of gunpowder that are released when a gun is fired.

UNIQUE PRINTS

The print examiner studies fingerprints, palm prints, and footprints found at a crime scene. These are then compared with the prints from any suspects and with prints found at other crime scenes. They are checked against a computer database of prints.

BACK AT THE LAB

The medical examiner (ME) is the person who decides the cause of death and oversees the analysis of evidence. If necessary, MEs appear in court to present their findings. The ME also supplies the police with the results of any forensic tests that have been performed.

EVIDENCE!

A crime scene is like a puzzle. Investigators collect the pieces (the evidence) and put them together to solve the crime.

ON TARGET

Investigators rarely find a gun at a crime scene, but they often find bullets. These can provide vital information, such as the make and model of the gun that fired them.

BLOODY TYPING

Blood found at crime scenes is examined by serologists. The red blood cells contain proteins called antigens. These determine a person's blood type and can help identify a killer as well as a victim. Antigens are either A or B. Someone with A antigens in their blood is called Type A. Someone with B antigens is Type B. People with both antigens are Type AB, and people with none are Type O.

A HEAD START

Hair is often found at crime scenes. If the hair follicle is still attached, it is possible to match the DNA. If not, hair can be examined to see if it contains any chemicals that are not usually found in people, such as poisonous substances.

INVISIBLE EVIDENCE

Fibers from clothes, carpets, and many other sources stick to skin, clothes, and hair. These fibers can be identified and matched to try to link the victim and suspect of a crime.

LEAVING PRINTS

If investigators are lucky, they will find fingerprints. These could be patent prints, which are found when a substance such as blood is transferred from a suspect's hand onto a surface. Latent prints cannot be seen by the human eye and require special lighting to be examined.

By measuring the dimensions of a bullet hole, scientists can establish the type of gun used.

Scientists test for antigens by mixing blood with Type A and B antibodies. For instance, if blood contains A antigens, it will clot when mixed with A antibodies. This match will establish that a person has Type A blood.

Numbered tags are used to mark where evidence, such as a bullet, is found at a crime scene.

Latent prints can be exposed with ultraviolet light.

THE TOOLS

At a crime scene, investigators have to discover, collect, and protect the evidence they find. Then they must transport it back to the lab. To do this job, they use a wide range of equipment.

plastic tube

TESTING FOR BLOOD

Every crime scene investigator carries a serology kit to test a scene for blood and other fluids that might contain DNA. Light sources (either ultraviolet or infrared) and the chemical luminol can be used to check for blood traces that are invisible to the naked eye.

EVIDENCE IDENTIFICATION

Date

Time

Case No

Test For
☐ DNA/SEROLOGY
☐ DRUGS
☐ FINGERPRINTS

☐ FIREARMS
☐ IMPRESSIONS
☐ QUESTIONED DOCUMENTS

☐ TOXICOLOGY
☐ TRACE EVIDENCE
☐ OTHER

Description of Evidence

Location Collected

☐ Found   ☐ Other

☐ Arrest   ☐ Seized

Victim/Incident

Remarks/Det

Agency

disposable glove

evidence tag

5

5

Along with gloves, investigators also wear disposable protective clothing, footwear, and masks. These make sure the investigators do not leave their own clothes, hair, and fingerprints at the crime scene.

cotton swab

evidence bag

EVIDENCE

CHAIN OF CUSTODY

magnifying glass

tweezers

PHOTOGRAPHING THE SCENE

A digital camera is a vital part of a crime scene investigator's equipment. Anything and everything is photographed and recorded, from the body to an overturned table or an uneaten meal. These photographs form an important part of the case file. They are often referred to when police are trying to spot clues they might have missed at the scene.

COLLECTING CLUES

To gather evidence, an investigator uses tweezers and cotton swabs for collecting hair, fiber, and fluids. A magnifying glass helps to spot the smallest bits of evidence. Everything is collected in plastic evidence bags and glass or plastic tubes to protect against contamination from outside sources.

DUSTING FOR PRINTS

The fingerprinting kit includes an ink pad, cards to print onto, and various dusting powders. Also in the kit are an exposing reagent (a chemical that shows up the oils present in fingerprints) and tape for lifting prints off surfaces such as door handles or a body.

MAKING CASTS

The casting kit is used to make molds. Tire tracks are called class evidence. This means that they can rule out certain car models but cannot absolutely identify a particular tire type. However, the tread mark of a shoe can identify its size and manufacturer. These are useful bits of evidence if police can trace the shoe to a purchase by a particular person.

dusting brush

dusting powder

15

A DNA SCIENTIST ON LIFE IN AND OUT OF THE LAB

DR. GEORGINA MEAKIN

THURS. JUNE 30, 2011

9 A.M. I work at a forensic institute. Defense attorneys from all over the country come to us when they need evidence in a case. This may involve re-examining old evidence or carrying out new DNA tests. My office hours are 9 to 5, but I have to be flexible. When attorneys are preparing a big court case, they work around the clock, and I have to be available too. That means weekends and evenings—whatever it takes to get the job done.

10 A.M. When I'm given a new case, the first thing I do is request all the case files, plus all the DNA and forensic tests. The lab is just ten minutes from my office, so I might walk over there, read through the files, and make my own notes. I'm usually back at my desk for lunch.

1 P.M. Sometimes I have to be in the lab carrying out DNA tests. At these times, I wear a standard white lab coat, rubber gloves, and a face mask to prevent any kind of contamination of evidence. But when I'm back at my desk, I can work on a case on my computer and eat lunch at the same time. You can't contaminate electronic data with a sandwich!

2 P.M. I specialize in DNA, so with each new case, I receive a CD of electronic DNA data. I load this onto a special software program on my computer that allows me to view the results. We don't analyze a person's entire DNA—that would take weeks—instead we just focus on 10 specific areas that are most often different among individuals.

6 P.M. I'm setting off for the airport. I have a court case down south tomorrow morning that could last several days. Attending court is part of my job, so I spend a lot of time in hotels. I'm in court on this occasion as an expert witness. I'll give written evidence, and then I may be asked to give evidence in the witness stand too. I haven't been in the witness stand yet. Colleagues say it is very stressful, but I'm looking forward to the challenge of it. It's all part of my job after all.

11 P.M. I check my e-mails one last time before it's time for bed. Court in the morning—I need to be fresh and ready to answer any questions if I'm needed.

HOOKED ON CSI

MY STORY BY CHRISTINA MARTIN

For as long as I can remember, I really wanted to study law. I loved all the courtroom dramas and CSI-type shows on TV and was fascinated by the legal process of finding and catching criminals. I decided to be a lawyer so that, one day, I would stand up in court and make my case to a jury.

In high school, I studied psychology, sociology, English, and law. After college, I was planning to go to law school. I really only wanted to study criminal law, but that wasn't possible in a law degree. Then my mom suggested I study forensic science. It was like a lightbulb had been switched on in my head. Of course! Why hadn't I thought of that before?

First, I took some basic classes in math and chemistry. Then I started on my undergraduate degree in forensic science. I had to take classes from all different departments—math, chemistry, biology, criminology, and even philosophy. I loved every minute—even the real autopsy we watched at the university hospital. The sight of blood—or worse—doesn't bother me. We studied everything from pathology to entomology. We even developed our own mock crime scene and gave evidence in a mock courtroom. Our teachers cross-examined us as though we were part of a real-life case.

I've just graduated and am looking for my first job. I'd love to work as a crime scene investigator, that would be my first choice, but I'm also interested in entomology and ballistics. I'd like to do different things and to have some variety in my work. Right now, I'm spending my days sending out résumés for every single forensic position that comes up. Wish me luck!

C. M

THE CRIME SCENE

You get the call at 2 A.M. As a fingerprint examiner, you are one of the first people the police call. Dragged from a deep sleep, you feel groggy but you splash some water on your face and jump in your car. Ten minutes later, you are at the crime scene. What you do from now on could be crucial to cracking this case and bringing the criminal to justice.

COVERING UP

You pull on your cleanroom suit to stop fibers from sticking to your clothes and other evidence contaminating the scene. The suit, hood, mask, and gloves can be uncomfortable and hot. You don't think you will ever get used to them!

FOCUSING ON THE SCENE

You duck under the tape to get to the crime scene. You are the first here—perfect for taking in everything and capturing events in your mind's eye. What happened in this room? Was it murder? An accident? Did the victim know his killer? The answers could be right here, in the evidence all around you.

DOWN TO BUSINESS

You get out your fingerprint kit. The powders come in a range of colors. You use the one that provides the greatest contrast with the background surface. The walls and woodwork here are white, so you choose black powder. You scan the doorframe and windowsill with your flashlight to try to pick up any sign of prints. You spot one by the door handle. A wave of excitement rushes over you. It could be the victim's. But with a bit of luck, it might be the killer's! You dust the print and examine it through a magnifying glass.

VALUABLE EVIDENCE

The print is a good quality result. First, your colleague takes a photo of it. Then you lift it. You lay a strip of sticky tape over the print, and then gently peel it off. You have done this hundreds of times before, but you can still feel the beads of sweat on your forehead. One wrong move and this print will be gone forever. Next, you lay the sticky tape onto a card, transferring the powder and the print. Done! Now it is back to the lab. Can you get a match on this print and help find the killer? This is what makes your job so exciting!

Plain whorls look like little whirlpools of ridge lines. They are found in 35 percent of the world's population.

Radial loops *(above)* are usually found on a person's index finger. They are less common than ulnar loops.

Just 5 percent of the world's population have arch prints.

RECOGNIZING FINGERPRINTS

Everyone has a unique set of fingerprints. Even identical twins have different fingerprints. There are three main types, with minor variations. This is how to spot them.

IN THE LOOP

The most common type of print is a loop—one or more ridge lines that double back on themselves. Loops are found on 60 to 70 percent of the world's population. Loops can be divided into two subgroups: radial loops and ulnar loops. Radial loops flow downward toward the thumb, and ulnar loops flow toward the little finger.

GOING AROUND IN CIRCLES

Whorls are circle-patterned prints that can be divided into four categories:

Plain whorls are the most common. They are either circular (like the rings on a dartboard) or spiral, which become smaller and smaller, like a wound spring.

Central pocket whorls look like a loop with a whorl at the end.

Double whorls include two separate loops that come together to form an S shape.

Accidental whorls are irregular, as the name suggests. Any whorl that does not fit in the three categories above is given this name.

RIDING THE WAVE

Arches are ridge lines that rise in repetition to create the shape of a wave. The arch pattern of lines is the least common of prints and was first recognized in 1926. There are two groups of arches. Tented arches have a more central rise (like the roof of a house or a tall mountain).

FIGHTING CYBER CRIME

Year after year, the number of people who use computers is rising. Not surprisingly, cyber crime is also on the increase. Computer forensic experts are trained to search for evidence that the rest of us do not even know exists.

Crimes organized on the Internet, such as terrorist strikes, are increasing every year.

HIDDEN DATA

Computers can be used for a range of crimes, from hacking (gaining illegal access to someone's computer to steal information) to fraud and even murder! Although many people believe that just pressing the delete key will get rid of evidence forever, that's not true. A computer simply allows you to write over that data, in the same way that you can put another coat of paint on a wall. The original information is still there—and an expert can find it.

THE EVIDENCE

Computer forensic experts look at the hard disk of a suspect's computer. They search for clues to the crimes the suspect is supposed to have committed. The information they retrieve helps to piece together the details of a suspect's actions—from the e-mails the person sent to the websites the person visited.

In 2009 Casey Anthony was arrested on suspicion of murdering her daughter. Computer forensic experts discovered that she used her home computer to search the Internet for the word *chloroform* (a powerful, dangerous drug) 84 times! But the evidence wasn't strong enough. Anthony was later found not guilty of the crime.

STOLEN GOODS

Computer forensic experts also use their skills to find the owners of stolen personal computers and laptops. Criminals wipe the hard disks clean. But special software allows experts to recover this hard disk information, providing valuable clues about the real owner of the computer. Because of their specialist knowledge, forensic experts are often required to appear in court as expert witnesses. As cyber crime increases, computer forensics is sure to be a growing area of the profession.

FAMOUS CASES

On the Radar examines some of the cases throughout history that have made news headlines and how they were solved by forensic experts.

1. POISONED?

Napoleon Bonaparte was the emperor of France from 1804 to 1815. After losing the Battle of Waterloo, he was exiled and died in prison in 1821. While in exile, Napoleon wrote to his friends saying that he was being poisoned. A few strands of his hair survived. When they were eventually tested in a forensic lab, they showed traces of the poison arsenic. But further research showed that food often contained high levels of arsenic during the time that Napoleon lived. The conclusion: he died of stomach cancer, not poisoning.

2. HAIR EVIDENCE

California-born Scott Peterson was found guilty of murdering his pregnant wife Laci in December 2002. Peterson reported his wife missing on Christmas Eve. Despite nationwide news coverage, she was not found. In April 2003, her body was washed ashore on a beach close to San Francisco, where Peterson often went sailing. On his boat, a single hair of Laci's was found in a pair of pliers. Peterson was convicted and is on death row.

3. CYBER CRIME

In June 2011, cyber detectives from Scotland Yard's e-crime unit arrested 19-year-old Ryan Cleary on suspicion of computer hacking. The teenager from Essex, England, is believed to be part of a group of hackers, who claim to be responsible for the cyber attacks on Sony's PlayStation 3 games system and the CIA's website. At the time of writing, Cleary is awaiting trial. If found guilty, he could be sent to the United States to serve his sentence.

4. TELLTALE FINGERPRINTS

In Seattle, Washington, in 1986, Stella Nickell's husband died of cyanide poisoning. The source was discovered to be a bottle of painkillers, which were contaminated with the poison. However, the police also discovered traces of a chemical found in fish tanks—like the one in Stella's house. Stella's daughter told the police that her mother had been researching the use of cyanide. At the local library, two books on poisons revealed traces of Stella's fingerprints! She was found guilty and sentenced to two 90-year terms in prison.

5. FAKE PAPERS

In 1983 the German journalist Gerd Heidemann announced that he had discovered the diaries of Adolf Hitler, who led Germany into World War II (1939–1945). The announcement sparked worldwide interest. *Newsweek* magazine agreed to buy the diaries for $3.74 million. However, when the forensic department of the German police force examined the diaries, they discovered that the ink used to write them had not been available during the war. The force also found the bleach that was used to whiten the paper did not exist until 1954—nine years after Hitler died. The diaries were fake!

DNA DATABASE FOR ALL?

FOR

Governments around the world hold DNA samples, usually from convicted criminals. These samples are used to solve crimes. There are calls for these databases to be expanded so that everyone's DNA is included. Supporters say:

1. DNA sampling is an important weapon in the fight against crime. These samples make it harder for criminals to get away with their deeds. The more DNA that is held on file, the more crimes will be solved.

2. If you have nothing to hide, then you don't need to be afraid of your DNA being included in a database.

3. The standard DNA test is very reliable. It compares samples in ten different ways—the likelihood of two unrelated people showing the same full DNA profile is one in a billion.

4. Familial DNA profiling—matching DNA profiles between members of the same family—can also help track down criminals. If just one member of a family is on the database, they can all be traced.

On the other hand, critics believe that DNA testing should not replace standard police work. They say:

AGAINST

1. DNA sampling can often provide inconclusive results. There have been thousands of cases of DNA samples found at crime scenes matching several people on a database at the same time.

2. Low copy number (LCN) DNA testing can create a DNA profile from just five or six cells, rather than the usual 200. This can make the DNA test much more unreliable. Many countries, including the United States, do not allow LCN evidence in court.

3. DNA samples can be passed from a guilty person to an innocent person by something as simple as just shaking hands or sitting in the same chair. Therefore, the results of DNA testing cannot be 100 percent accurate.

4. An innocent person's DNA could be planted at a crime scene, either to mislead police or to transfer blame to someone else.

5. DNA testing is expensive, and money is being spent in this area while other areas of police work, such as patrolling high crime areas, are neglected.

Right or wrong?

DNA testing helps catch criminals. But it shouldn't become the only method that the police use. And it shouldn't mean that everyone in a country should be made to give a DNA sample. New technology and scientific breakthroughs can be game changers, but people's freedom of choice is also important.

FORENSIC FIGURES

99.9

The percentage of DNA that is the same in every person.

1835

The first time that forensics was used to match a bullet taken from a victim, with the gun that fired it.

1

The percentage of people in the world with an AB blood type—the rarest blood group.

37

The percentage of people in the world with an O+ blood type, the most common blood group.

1858

The year that the first recorded set of fingerprints was taken.

12,996

The number of people murdered in the United States in 2010.

1,250

The approximate number of days spent identifying victims of the 9/11 disaster in New York City in 2001.

80

The percentage of victims who can usually be identified by dental records after an explosion or mass disaster.

All figures provided are from 2010 records.

GET MORE INFO

Further Reading

Brown, Jeremy. *Four-Minute Forensic Mysteries: Body of Evidence*. New York: Scholastic Books, 2006. These fictional stories have a forensic team heading out to all kinds of mysterious crime scenes to try to solve the case.

Cooper, Chris. *Forensic Science*. New York: Dorling Kindersley, 2008. Using pictures and text, this book explains the tools and methods forensic scientists use to crack the case.

Fridell, Ron. *Forensic Science*. Minneapolis: Lerner Publications Company, 2007. Learn the history of forensic science and how forensic science is practiced.

Stefoff, Rebecca. *Famous Forensic Cases*. Salt Lake City: Benchmark Press, 2008. Discover how forensics were used to solve some puzzling and famous crime investigations.

Websites

Discovery Channel
http://investigation.discovery.com/interactives/interactives.html
Play these forensic games to learn more about crime scene investigations.

Montréal Science Center
http://www.centredessciencesde montreal.com/static/autopsy/index.htm
Use this website to perform an interactive murder investigation that takes you from the crime scene to the laboratory.

PBS American Experience
http://pbs.org/wgbh/amex/dillinger/sfeature/sf_whodunit.html#
At this interactive website, solve a bank robbery using fingerprints.

INDEX